WOMEN & OTHER HOSTAGES

WOMEN & OTHER HOSTAGES

Laura McCullough

www.blacklawrence.com

Executive Editor: Diane Goettel
Cover Design: Zoe Norvell
Cover Art: "Lady of Snakes" by Kyle Mosher
Book Design: Amy Freels

Published 2021 by Black Lawrence Press.
Printed in the United States.

Heart, you bully, you punk, I'm wrecked, I'm shocked...
Marie Ponsot

Contents

Prologue

MEDUSA AS A PARABLE OF FAITH
    & RESILIENCE   3

I
Women & the Syntactical World

COUGAR ME THIS   11
EMOTICONFISCATED   12
CREDIT RATING   14
WOMEN & THE SYNTACTICAL WORLD   16
UNTIL YOU KNOW IT   19
CHILDREN & THE PARTICULATE LIGHT   20
SWEET SICK   21
SOME LINGUISTS SEE SYNTAX AS A
    BRANCH OF BIOLOGY   22
SWORN VIRGIN   24
IN THE GARDEN OF MEN   25
WOMEN & THE NATURAL WORLD   26
BENEFICIAL INSECTS   27
THE PUBLIC POOL ON POINT   28
HEAT & SHAME   30
LISTENING FOR SNOW   31

II
Other Hostages

WOMEN & OTHER HOSTAGES   35
WOMEN & OTHER FEMALE
    IDENTIFICATIONS   37

WORK & NOISE 38

WATER LINE 40

SOLID & VOID 42

YOU HAVE TO BECOME STONE 43

POEM WITH THE WORD 'DAMAGE'
      FOUR TIMES (DX4) 45

BIOLOGY LESSON: APPROPRIATION
      OF THE LOVER 46

WHAT COMES OUT OF THE SKY AT A
      HORIZONTAL TRAJECTORY 47

THE PLACES WE HAVE ALL BEEN 48

III
The Owls of Mercy & Grace

ICARUS IN THE HOUSE OF SPIRITS 51

THE TROUBLES OF MEN: HOLOMETABOLY 52

THE OWLS OF MERCY & GRACE 54

HUNGER & SNAKE 55

WALKING PALMS UP IN THE DARK 56

JUNIPER 57

SATELLITES: PERMANENT ONLY
      IN MEMORY 59

THE WATER INSISTS ON TAKING
      EVERYTHING 61

CURVE OF FORGETTING 62

DISSONANCE & STILL 63

TRAFFIC & CONSTRUCTION 64

EVERYONE IS WHAT 66

MOLECULARITY 67

IV
Marriage

(trajectories)   71
(skin)   71
(intergenerational wounds)   72
(water)   72
(wood & dog)   73
(after unseen damage from the flood)   73
(stew)   74
(roots)   74
(the re-articulation)   75
(woman with two hearts)   75
(how to hold a heart)   76
(more than mercy)   76
(what they try in spring)   77
(being in becoming)   77
(motel)   78

V
Fallen Kingdoms

A Guide to Wild Flowers   81
THE LOGIC OF YOU   82
KINGDOM OF CLASS   83
THE WILL   84
MUSIC IN THE KINGDOM OF THE HEART   85
Bonne Chute (good falling)   87
HEAT   88
ALMOST NOTHING SOMETHING
        [stars / plates / cells]   90

Acknowledgments   93
Gratitudes   95

Prologue

MEDUSA AS A PARABLE OF FAITH & RESILIENCE

Birth, not death, is the hard loss.
I know. I also left a skin there.
Louise Glück

Pain is joy when it cries, it's my smile in disguise.
Pusha T

1.
Sometimes mistakes are set
          to right; others never are.
                    Athena never owned up
to her crime against Medusa.

We know what Poseidon did
          to her & how
                    Medusa was blamed for it.
Athena had daddy issues & competed

with other women,
          her projections & rage
                    transforming Medusa
into a monster as punishment for the crime

of having been raped.
          Even women blame
                    the victim.   I've always loved
snakes, those in the grass or on the path,

misunderstood & mis-cast;
  they are victims, too.
    I've heard this joke:
He'd even screw a snake if someone pinned it down.

2.
I've been teased
  my head is full
    of snakes, hair wild,
a thistle brush, rarely pretty, always too much.

Snakes & curls
  have a lot in common;
    & girls aren't always your friends;
Poseidon was a bastard, & maybe Athena was

jealous of Medusa,
  but the punishing
    had its gifts. What is stripped
from you—skin of identity—lets you choose:

accept the shadow & glow,
  wet, raw, vulnerable:
    if someone steals from you,
what's left behind is all you own, like Medusa's blood

became medicine.
  Asclepius revived a snake;
    it whispered secret knowledge
of healing into his listening ear—the rod of this god

has one snake coiled;
   considered divine,
     a being wise, its wreathed body
a symbol of bringing people back from the dead.

3.
All these gods & goddesses!
   Fucking whomever they could
     pin down, or fucking someone
up or over, mortal or immortal, kids jumping out of heads

or broken earth, being
   raised by snakes or
     like the snake,
discovering both their poison & ability to shed skin—

like the father wound,
   mother grief—disappointments
     & betrayals both flaying
us alive & renewing us. When I say, all my life my hair

was my bane,
   my shame,
     an accusation & a curse,
I am saying there was pain in the becoming.

4.
You who broke
   my heart, I didn't turn
     to stone. Grotesque,
maybe, my coarse tangled mess, these snakes

are more wondrous
        as I age, & my blood
                holds both pain & joy.
You remember that, don't you? Pain is joy? Pusha T

knows poison like
        Glück knows isolation.
                Do you de-fang dis?
        Or dine off it?   No one
can be believed anymore.   Not one
        of the gods can be pinned down,

        & my hair gets frizzier by the day.
Like snake skin, the latter shed, mine
        gets redder, both penny bright & gray.

        My head is roiling snake charmed
& only half fro'd out,
just a type 3B or C, curly not coil—
        judged by elasticity, variance, & porosity.

5.
I'm going to read Glück's
        Meadowlands backwards,
                & her parable thus:

        In pain as in joy.
        In the generous heart

I'm going to twist my hair, pinch my snakes, release their poison:

        The grief of his lady: his
        Yet gladly would the king bear

Or maybe I'll just pardon the world,
             as if it were possible
                          to do so before I'm dead,
but maybe after, my blood,
             one drop damning, the other reviving,
             feuding with itself, embodied
by these knots, these *Caduceusized* matted,
             near dreads, still unlocked
             either to be cut out or embraced.

I choose neither pain nor joy,
             nothing about the night that's virtuous,
             just necessary, no perfect endings,
             only endings & endings, & endings
             as Glück said.   Shall I feed—
             as others fed off me—these snakes

instead of a snake in the grass as Virgil first wrote—
oh herd-boys picking flowers & strawberries, beware
the cold snake lurking in the grass—or just cut off

their heads
             (whose head?) or shave my own?

Or just follow the map of my hair into the night
             of grief
             & grievance?   Or slough off

even the concepts of truth or justice,
             embrace the ouroboros,
             the snake eating its own tail.

I
Women & the Syntactical World

COUGAR ME THIS

Men are afraid of her, they say,
                     but what is there to fear? What men
                     have always desired & then despised,

the woman who wants it, who hunts,
                     whose muscular, sexual psyche
                     wafts over the room pheromonally,

clinging, dangerous. She's on the loose.
                     Who knows what will be left
                     when the morning fog lifts?

Flesh, certainly, since she doesn't feed for hunger.
Bones that are not worth carrying away.

Such falseness,
           this,
                     like an old movie.

But after the movie, as you walk out from safety
                     into the wide, wide open night,
                     listen to what growls in the dark.

                     Feel the changing texture of the night.

                     Longing's residue collects on the vegetation;
                     it is what indicts & endangers you

& what you can't live without.

                     Tilt back your neck; expose your throat.
                     You know you want to be devoured.

EMOTICONFISCATED

It was me on Cookman Ave. that night
the newscaster was in the news
for what apparently everyone had always known,
& the man I was with was making me feel—
what? I asked him, actually asked him, *My god,
what are you making me feel?*   He was holding
me in his arms; we'd been kissing.   Okay,

I'll just say it; we were *mashing* like teenagers,
as people who used to think this is all
teenagers do would say, & we'd been
interrupted by a passerby, a younger woman
by decades. *I just want to know
if you are okay & this is consensual,* she said.

I hadn't been kissed in close to a year then,
& I was so okay, blisteringly, my amygdala firing—
fear, it seems, is sexy—& I tried
to tell her I was *fine, yes, thank you, what a moment
in social time we are in,* & she went away,
& I asked him again, *What are you making me feel?*
& he whispered,

                    desirable.
                    I wanted to hide

my face in shame; I wanted to run
naked in the moist & glittering street. I wanted
to know how he must have felt to be holding

a woman with the bold strength of his body
allowing mine to soften & shiver,

our breathing in each other this way
wakening the monsters we fear
but need, as well, surrender not just about having
something taken from us but about giving up.

      I swear,   where we stood
in the lonely & suspicious night,
      we must have left evidence
           of what we had seized & taken
possession of, or what had possessed us,
      scorch marks on the concrete
      for anyone to see,   if only they'd look.

CREDIT RATING

She has none, my friend,
   who understands the influence
   of Brecht on Benjamin
& why rhetoric matters in poetry
& also what it means to lose her credit cards,
   to live by cash,

& how to talk
   to faceless faces of the corporate entities
   that want to eat her alive,
how much to offer,
how much to hold back. She loves Benjamin

who made up the term *auratic perception*,
   meaning ways in which a culture
   reclaims a mythology for itself,

& she undercuts the corporate gods
   by using cash only.

Each day, an angel of god
   in the voice of an Accounts Receivable Representative
   calls my friend's cell,
   a ritual.
They think she is waiting for some kind of absolution
   for the sin of economic collapse—

the original sin we all apparently have been reborn with—

& later will field calls from other account representatives
    offering her new credit cards:
    how else to regain your rating?
    Remain part of the flock?

WOMEN & THE SYNTACTICAL WORLD

Would it help to know
    I'm a little in love
        with your husband?

        Or that I'm in love

with my own, &
    I'm not going anywhere?
        Or that the version of me

        you hear in this poem

is a version of me
    that loves mostly poets,
        a few artists, one tile guy,

        & a couple of older

doctors, including
    William Carlos Williams
        whom a lot of women loved

        & a lot of men have loved,

as well? If he—
    & now I'm speaking
        of your husband—loved

        me, say, outside by those falls,

the one hard to find
    in the city, it only
        would have enlarged us both.

        There is that one letter written

as a poem about cell
    division as a metaphor
        for communication, but my news

        for you is that all poems

are love poems
    in my book. Can I kiss you?
        your tongue standing

        in for his tongue, your ear

delicious in its resistance.
    I ask only because I want
        to sidle up to the hips

        of this world, bend it

over at the waist, check
    the small bones of its back,
        whisper into the concaves,

        Oh forgive me, forgive me.

I've tried to hide this,
    keep my mouth closed,
        but the world pried me open

        long ago, & I chose not to fight

back, selecting instead,
   the pleasure of giving
      in to what I can't explain

    & simply won't apologize for.

UNTIL YOU KNOW IT

It was the winter I was stomping around the house
complaining about your love being too good for me,
& what if all the other women found out,
they'd be lined up down the block,
& you were scoffing, of course,
that little V between your brows
getting more like a V every year.

You surprised me one day with a CD
of my favorite singer-songwriter.
It was the first music we'd shared in a while,
& I tried to be a better wife.
For your birthday, I bought you a shirt
the shade of raspberry sherbet,
thinking you needed some color
& you looked lovely, that little V breaking up
like geese forgetting they're flying south.

Sometimes, while you sleep, I touch that space,
smoothing & memorizing it
while planning my next transgression,
hoping it won't be what you'll finally leave me over,
like the last song in a great album,
the one that makes you cry & listen
over & over until you know it so well,
you don't need the music anymore.

CHILDREN & THE PARTICULATE LIGHT

All squabble light, bright shafts blowing out of fingertips
& coronas circling their heads,
these vultures of soul,
despite our best un-intentions,
the television only one sin,
then the portable everything.

Frannie said it's not the self, but soul that matters,
& all this catering to self,
infighting between us,
is just a waste of time.

The circle of screaming light dancing about your head,
I know it matters, but today,
all I want to do is feed you,
again, & then put you to bed,
silence coming down around me,
so I can put out the damned light.

SWEET SICK

There, next to me in bed,
her small hand on mine,
the other one tucked in her blanket,
the one I keep trimming, the one growing smaller,
I think she looks diminished, all watery & loose,
but I am disheveled, not a proper mother,
my hair frazzled like some painter stroked red
where my head should be;
we're a pair, bedded by flu,
but since she's only four, she doesn't understand,
knows only the TV is on, & we're coughing together,
& no one's going anywhere.
One of her hands is larger than the other;
there's a name for that sort of limb discrepancy,
but who cares? Right now, she couldn't pronounce it
even if I could recall it,
but she unwinds her fingers from the blanket holes
they slept in & puts that hand on my face
& cups the bone beside my eye.
You're hot again, mama, she says,
but her eyes are pleased.
Everything is an arrow
from the bow of this moment.

I take her two hands & kiss each of them.
I haven't been this gloriously sick in years.

SOME LINGUISTS SEE SYNTAX AS A
BRANCH OF BIOLOGY

Let's talk about vaginas, she says
      after her shower & spread-eagles

on the fluffy green mat, her feet
      at odd angles over her shoulders,

the moisture obscuring the reflection
      I look at to see how aghast I might

actually be, but all I say is *Okay,*
      & hand her a small, cracked, concave

mirror. She is looking at her holes,
      transfixed in wonder, wanting to know

what they are for & why hers are little
      & mine so big. Transudation is the word

for wetness, the kind that comes from
      the walls of that famous cellar, the vagina,

words rooted in mind, fecund & dangerous
      where things both rot & grow. She asks

What is this bump for? I say, *Your clitoris,*
      but don't explain what I know about it.

At the dinner table, she asks her father,
      & he says, *There's a reason we call*

these private parts, & she says, *Yes,*
	& only mommies & daddies share

them, & maybe girlfriends & boyfriends
	who really like each other. She pauses,

Or just married mommies & daddies?
	& this is now a question not a statement,

& her daddy says, *Yes,* emphatically,
	Yes, honey, to me now, his eyes relaying

the order of his thoughts, *Six today, fifteen*
	tomorrow, & I don't look back at him,

but pull my girl onto my lap & say,
	Let's talk about bones, & run my hand

along her spine. She smiles, *Yes, bones,*
	mommy, bones. She arches her back, *I want*

to know everything you can tell me about them
	& I look down at my forearms around her

& twist them this way, thinking *tibia, ulna.*
	That's all I know, nothing else, not why or

how they work or the density that dissolves
	over time, the fragility to come, & instead

I say, *Birds' bones are hollow, one reason*
	they can fly; our heavy bodies hold us down.

She perches on me now like a bird, her
	knees on mine, face tilted, wide & waiting.

SWORN VIRGIN

I could never have been Queen Elizabeth,
but there's always been a way to transgress
into the garden of men
where women have little luck or power
unless they lay down,
roll over, do the tending.

Who wants to be a gardener
if you could stand there with the other flowers
erect, facing the sun, deciding the fate of bees?
Do aphids have a queen?
No, & they change sex as necessary,
sometimes many times a season,
& some are winged & others not,
& inside a female is the body of another female
growing the body that will be the granddaughter.

In the garden, aphids swarm the flowers,
eating sap or phloem,
vectors for viruses, & can wipe out a garden.
The god of the garden, bi-legged & fixed in gender
swears to kill them before they migrate,

but you can be sure they cling with six two jointed legs
to whomever's pant legs they can,
immune to royalty's lure.

IN THE GARDEN OF MEN

A field of men like flowers waiting for harvest,
men like gladiolas, tall, florid, spiked, & coming
in all colors. We women race among them, gathering
them in our arms, dipping our faces into them. Once,
I passed a farm fence—fences are so important—
& there she was, nothing much to set her apart,
but the heat of her thick in the humid, country air
as she rolled her rump against a post. You know
what she needed. She had a field, empty but for grass,
& don't we all want more than just enough space
& a good feed? Two feet, arms free to embrace,
the heat in a low slung spine, the way it bends like
flowers in a stiff wind all the way to the ground.

WOMEN & THE NATURAL WORLD

She calls today to say the baby came early
& it's nothing like she imagined,

no surprise because it never is.
There is no perfect time to have a baby,

no way to anticipate the widening boney aperture
of childbirth, no time right to go to war.

Some insects like the tachinid fly parasitize
the larvae of beetles, eating the offspring of others,

a thing wise gardeners exploit to protect
what they've planted. When she calls me,

she says, *There's never been a baby as beautiful as this,*
& I say, *Yes, yes,* but a spring, like a coiling proboscis

clicks tight in my mind, *Oh, yes there has.*
I can see my daughter on her computer;

I can hear my mother behind me calling out,
My beautiful girl. The new mother on the phone

thanks me for my wise advice. *It's nothing,* I say,
women haven't always done for each other.

She hasn't a clue what's coming, what this love does,
what ways we find to eat each other from the inside out.

BENEFICIAL INSECTS

Not the greenhead though the female lays her eggs
on beetle larvae, friend to gardeners, but if you're a beetle,

very bad & for beach goers or anyone outdoors
in the humid, salty-aired Pines of Jersey for six weeks,
two terrible ones in late June.

She is monstrous with her huge, beautifully metallic
head, wings folded tight against her carapace.

Where are the males? Dozing, no bite to them,
just the gals winged phlebotomists,
leaving welts the size of silver dollars.

The trick is to let her insert the needle,
then, in the moment of your piercing,

in her unfathomable shift in alien consciousness
from the stick to the suck,
you strike, amazed at the weight of her dumb body as it falls.

Somewhere another female lays ugly
& safe, no shine, no glow, easy to ignore,

to forget her capacity to sting,
to not even know she exists in this world
or that she will stab you when she can.

THE PUBLIC POOL ON POINT

Maryann recounts how her son nearly drowned
   the day before
& the day before that, the choking incident.
   I just want some control back in my life.
I laugh, not meaning to be cruel, but can't help it.

My head aches, guts shot,
   scared & sore & sour & mad
   at the ultra rich
   with their tattooed make-up, collagen & glycolics,
   their bio-sculpting this & that,
   their perfect *on fleek* eyebrows,

& all I want is to lie down,
   my morning mantra, *Is it bed time yet?*

I am tired   of *the drowning child,*
         the sick father,
         the depressed friend.   Maryann
is near tears now, & I pat her arm,

wondering if this is how America got where it is,
   drunk with fear & desire to stave it off
   by having everything:
      the big car,
      big house,
      big fence to enclose it all,
      big medicine to keep death at bay.
How much we spend to look immortal.

Maryann's eyes are big & dark
        like a cornered animal's.

I smell the fear on our skin.

HEAT & SHAME

A married man. Bearded, but with a newspaper
flipped up against his face. A doctor, too.
TMI, he cries. We're in bathing suits, his wife & I.

She's perfect & small, fecund with her own griefs
& hard-won openness. Me, I'm in a two piece,
belly slack & tattooed from childbirth.

We're talking about estrogen, blood & its lack.
Please, he whimpers. Without a word, we stand up
together & look down at him, suddenly cruel.

Our arms akimbo, nostrils flared like horses,
this is a pleasure we can't or don't wish to resist;
who would want to give up this power or lose it?

LISTENING FOR SNOW

It was just one of those days when your body
is suddenly all you have,

& you're afraid
you're going to misplace it or that it's being

slowly stolen right out from under your nose.
Don't look at me

like that, I said to him;
I'm so ugly; can't you see how it's all falling

apart? He smiled. *Oh,* he said, *you're as beautiful
to me now as ever.*

I could only touch
the line of his beard, reassuring as it's always been,

like walking in the woods on a fall day, the way
the wind smells

when you kick up
the browned leaves, all relief & promise, how things

falling apart only make something new. He touched
the curve of my waist,

the hollows near
my spine. Winter was coming; I listened to the snow

clouds giggling
like girls, frail, transitory, but preparing to be cruel.

II
Other Hostages

WOMEN & OTHER HOSTAGES

Everyone seemed stuck or silenced that summer,   nobody's
T-shirt with the right slogan, the news shifting   so fast, you

couldn't keep up with the latest outrage, & one person's outrage

was another's fact, & did you know   any couples
who weren't fighting or divorcing, or confused   over the kids,

the economy, the government? *Vulnerable* was a word I heard

in the grocery store as well as on the beach.   *Wild* was
a word I heard used as a positive & a negative.   I agreed

with everyone. When Bernard said there is no such thing

as morality out of context, I had to forgive him   because
I knew he'd be the last to leave the party,   would cry

in my driveway, was sorry for all the pain he'd caused

people he loved, didn't know how it   had happened,
but that it wasn't his fault; he was hostage   to the gender

constructs of his time. Many of us wished for a way to talk

about these things. Most everyone had some   private grief;
me, too couldn't sustain its slogan power   because everyone

had a version if you were willing to listen. A lot of men

got taken down. A lot of women felt ashamed   for liking men.
Did any of us know what was happening?   Whenever possible

I told people they were beautiful—in their bodies, their cages

of mind, under their habits of behavior—even in the   licks of fear
behind their corneas, something fluttering, a   grace, maybe mercy,

morally unambiguous. *Bernard*, I said, *I love you out of context,*

& if I say now that I almost meant it,   meaning I want
to be just a bit ironic, know instead that I am lying: I did mean it.

I really did. Even if someone else might think that's wrong

of me. Some days I think all I am capable of is   putting my hand
on someone's chest or shoulder, feeling the ridge of   rib bone or clavicle

against my palm, steadying myself there & giving a fee

to the ferryman's heart inside, wondering if we all   are trying
to escape from the shore of ourselves to   whatever waits

on the other side, feeling we have to help each other,

but knowing nothing, not even the forces   to which I
was pledged as hostage before I was born   & still act out

like the dumb beautiful beast I am occasionally thrilled to be.

WOMEN & OTHER FEMALE IDENTIFICATIONS

My mother used to say, a beautiful woman   makes men
feel handsome, but a truly beautiful woman   makes other women

feel beautiful. It was a graceful & affirmative idea

to have implanted in me as a girl, though cis-het   in its framing,
forgivable given the times though it still has   power, & I tell

women all the time that they are beautiful including

a woman with vivacious gray curls & a bouncing gait I saw
in the Acme parking lot today. But that's not why   I'm thinking

of it. I'm feeling the memory of you in my throat,

the way you surrendered & shuddered,   stunned
by the softness that came over you, though   few would have

thought me the one in power if they'd been watching

through a curtain crack. My mother used to say,   *Grace*
is seeing in someone's face the child   *they once were.*

& after, your jaw loosened, & that look as you laid back

was like an angel's or a child's, & I knew   you
were both grateful & ashamed, & maybe   a little afraid.

WORK & NOISE

Before I cross the tracks into Asbury,   at the circle
where accidents happen often, the white van   announces

INMATE LABOR PROGRAM

& the men, all BIPOC & young—meaning   not one has anything
white or gray on their heads or faces,   in their orange

striped work suits—stand

in the Jersey shore humidity in a week   social media
declares as hottest on record globally.   I'm going

to lunch with an old friend

to discuss the mythology of our time   & our shames.
Griefs. Grievances. Console ourselves   about all

we've endured. Learned.

We're amazing aren't we? After, I won't   go back
through that circle. It's embarrassing.   But I'll sit

at the strip mall on a bench

in the heat but under an awning.   Stamped
concrete faux cobblestone makes the   shopping

carts raucous. Three different women

will apologize to me as they push by,   sorry
they are disturbing what they think   is my peace.

As if I deserve it. As if it's my birthright.

WATER LINE

Live watching the Malibu Beach tide come in,   feeling
close to my friend Beth helps assuage the   sorrow

I felt when Jordan posted the Tampa Trump Rally pics

of strangers belonging to the family of fear &   outrage
even though they might have been feeling   some kind

of tide was washing over them. This fear of drowning

seems pervasive in the culture, though few will   admit
the causes, which usually have to do with   things

having nothing to do with what's going on right now,

things forgotten or too complex & no one likes   to feel
dumb in this culture of test taking &   economic

system revisioning

      & you got revisioned right out

of that arm chair pension you'd been promised   way back
when college wasn't an option for you anyway,   so you agree

it's the *damned immigrants taken over are cuntry,*

                                           a sign seen

at the rally Jordan attended, & I like the Malibu   rocks better,
& that Beth was getting her iPhone way down   by the water

line, so it felt like I was there, almost, & the sound

was like I could almost feel those negative ions   in the air.
        Except I'm not there—

        I'm thinking about *you*—

but the simultaneity felt   real,
& so I'm paradoxically feeling angry   & enlivened

by politics & nature. As if they aren't   connected.
We know they are; everything is.   Those dumb

rocks are made of the same star dust as my sign-carrying cousin

in Florida's beating fist, the one he pounds   his chest
with then raises in the air. His fist is   white. The rock

is gray. Jordan is Muslim, trying to pass, so he can record what

happens, so folks like me who aren't there   can see the tide
coming, the raging tide coming in,   the waves

that might even envelope him if he's not careful, & we

can know what it's like, something we couldn't   believe
if we weren't seeing it, thanks to someone   at the water line,

risking getting wet for the rest of us at home, safe & dry.

SOLID & VOID

Some mornings I wake, & I'm close
to some understanding. With it comes
not a peace precisely, but a small shiver
          of aloneness & acceptance
          of one's inconsequence.
                    Then I ask myself why
I dedicate so much time, indeed wake
instantly into, thinking about people.
What they do. What they need.
          How I hurt
them or fell
          short. How they hurt me
or fell short.
                    I'm alive.
& I enjoy my sheets for a minute. The sound
of an open window.

Then I remember I've become
used to sleeping with half read
or half absorbed books, split spines
strewn around me. I was thinking
while the birds filled the morning void
that your needs for attachment are different
from mine, & about the big crimson flashlight
you gave me
          when you left, the one I use
to prop open a book at night,
          to keep it
                    from fluttering closed
on my chest.

YOU HAVE TO BECOME STONE

A more defended exterior will enable the dazzling interior to survive.
—Charles Simic

The woman massaging my hand with expertise & talent
          & kindness
          is surprised when I begin to cry. There is a table
between us no wider than a foot. If we wanted
to touch
knees, we could.   She's done my nails. An unnatural
color called Lotus Sky. The salon owner is Vietnamese.
This woman is Latinx; she struggles with English, & I have
almost no Spanish, but my hand is in her hand,
          & when I start to cry, so does she.

There is something we know

about each other.   A friend

texted that one has to become stone
          in order not to become stone. I can hardly say
that in English.   Later, I will learn
that the woman who has held my hand
in a way I can never recall it being held before
studied as a massage therapist before
she came here from wherever she came from.

It is rude to ask. What I want to ask
is, how many days will you need to work here
until you can do what you studied to do? What
money would it take to get you out of here?
          I don't have any money to give her,
but I tip well. They always greet me
with enthusiasm.

Once, I told a friend
I only get my nails done when I'm depressed.
Now I can't imagine my own nails anymore.

What I like is this: a scar runs down my thumb,
the nail cloven. The women here make it
          look perfect,
like all the rest   & also this public
sanctioned touching, intimacy with clear boundaries.

When I start to cry, I know I've broken the rules,
& rush to tell her it's nothing
she is doing, it's just
this life.   When she starts to cry, as well,
I'm both ashamed & also wildly
& inexplicably hopeful for us all.

POEM WITH THE WORD 'DAMAGE' FOUR TIMES (DX4)

The day he told me, I punched a wall
with my left hand,   not my right.
I don't know why, since it is the weaker one,
after all, & capable of less damage.
I hadn't wanted to hit him nor do damage,
but the grief went through me like a bomb
dropped in a river, the water displaced
as if by lightning strike. He was sorry,
of course, but said he was trapped on a path
he saw no way off of, & there was no saving
him, he said, which I wouldn't have been strong
enough to do anyway,   arrogance

one of the lessons I had begun to learn
              about myself.   We'd been two hands
of a couple. Enmeshed they call it now. Fairy tale
love. Doomed from the start. Today someone told me
they don't believe in redemption nor forgiveness.
*What's done is done. You move on. It's the right
side of things,* she said   *But I like*

the left, I said, *Maybe all I've ever believed in
is redemption & forgiveness.*   *A weakness*, she said,
in me.
              This hand, long after:
It still aches sometimes, & when I put pressure
on it, feel a little pain in the wrist
              as if it's never quite healed, as if
it's never quite forgiven me for what
              I did to it.

BIOLOGY LESSON: APPROPRIATION OF THE LOVER

My tenth grade teacher stood with one long-fingered hand
        inside the chest cavity of a real skeleton,
        her nails caressing the rib bones,

& I saw the body's rebar was articulated
        with hooks, screws, & springs,
        the largest through the spine & skull
        resting its elegant curve
        on the rolling hanger from which he/she/they hung,

but it felt as if I saw one person's hand inside another's body,
& the idea in me ignited that there were ways to enter someone
        that I hadn't yet heard about. Beneath my shirt,

I knew what pounded
        & knew, too, that what the body wanted,
        it would get, though I had no idea what
        anything was, only that there was a wild
        night inside me.   A poet said, you only have

to let the soft animal of your body love what it loves,

        but no, that's not enough,   & reckless.

After some living, who hasn't felt flayed
        alive, skinned to the bone, & left to sky burial
        by someone their body loved?   Who hasn't put
        their hand beneath someone's rib & squeezed,
        desire the excuse they wear like skin?

WHAT COMES OUT OF THE SKY AT A HORIZONTAL TRAJECTORY

Through the transparency
of glass that keeps out the heat & cold
but lets light in,
the boy & the father lay together, faces
nestled, each partly in shadow
partly in the shine of the half moon,
its own darkness still its own for days to come.
Their faces. The heat of them. The letting down,
the reaching, the pulling up their legs,
knees bending, the boy's over his father's,
not rooting, not
trying, just being
like
the duo of silent herons I see beyond them
now passing overhead,
swimming through the air on their way
from where they were
to where they must go.

THE PLACES WE HAVE ALL BEEN

My neighbor is selecting paints
from the sale rack at Home Depot,
small rejected containers,
finger prints of the colors inside
that weren't quite right—indigo instead
of cerulean, blush instead of carmine.
After two tours in Iraq, he has a companion
dog who goes with him everywhere.
Lately, he's been painting birdhouses
he sells on Etsy for $19.99.
I think about the choices we all make
& about made & salvaged things.
As I watch, he lays down on the floor
of the aisle & embraces his dog.

Once I would have looked away
or taken my cart to another aisle,
but instead watch, & what ripples in my body
isn't fear or loneliness but makes me want
to get down on my knees & beg
for something, for me, for us all.

III
The Owls of Mercy & Grace

ICARUS IN THE HOUSE OF SPIRITS

In the Great Swamp, he described the most common owls—
Screech, Great Horned, Barred. He pointed to the sky
where a tangle of black birds swooped & called. Even I
could see how angry they were. *That's 'mobbing'*,
he said. *They're trying to scare a Great Horned out.*
He swore the owl was above, but I couldn't look up
without getting dizzy.   Looking now

in the bathroom mirror
            in Asbury Park's Johnny Mac's House of Spirits,
                            I remember
holding his hand,
        the sound of the screaming
                        birds drilling inside my skull.
The faces surrounding my reflection are all women's—
brown, pale, nutty, speckled—all primping & preening,
peacocked & prettified, a lovely & terrifying flock

of which I am part.
                        I can't recall
his face, but his hands
I can in detail—shape of palm, meat of thumb, bent of fingers—
as if they were wing shoots holding him above

the sorrows of his life, out of reach of what chased him,
& I can feel the bird-heart in my chest fluttering

while my face seems hollowed,
owlish in this dim light in which we hope
to confirm our beauty.

THE TROUBLES OF MEN:
HOLOMETABOLY

One restroom at Club Taboo, Asbury Park is gender free,
though it was once the Ladies room
& so has stalls with doors, no urinals,

& enough sink room for lots of us to preen against
the mirror.   Everyone leans to pluck
hair up or over, pull clumped eyelashes,

pucker mouths & frown. Someone says, *Honey, I just have to
have that lipstick,* & reaches for it.
She's right; when she slides it across

her lip, then blows a kiss at the mirror, it's as if her mouth
was meant to be this color,
do that thing. Someone recorded

sounds inside a chrysalis; magnified, they are wrenching, like wood
being chipped, a disintegrating tree
trunk, a chain saw to a door,

rain on a metal roof. A micro-ct rendered in 3-D reveals the pupa
dissolves from what it was
into a protein soup,

then slowly reconstitutes into what it will become. Outside this
room, the music is a cocoon
we all will writhe inside,

but I linger at this mirror watching faces come & go. Sometimes
a cis-male comes in thrilled
because he can, because

no one tells him to leave. He looks at everyone. We share that,
this looking. Sometimes
he even looks at himself.

THE OWLS OF MERCY & GRACE

They sing in different trees, the trees
still root into the earth held together
with soil & invisible sentience—fungi,
bacteria—& the air & ground falling
in love & fighting all the time. Here,
we tread, bottom feeders of the air, topdogs
of the soil. How did we lose everything?
Is memory that insufficient? I am willing
to hear the owls in the distance as they call,
but isn't there also the sound of cows low-
lowing their song, needing to be milked
or reunited with a lost calf or who knows
what? To have mercy is to forgive despite
a deserved punishment; grace is being given
something even though we don't deserve it.
We can be the bestowers of mercy or grace
or the receivers. Like the four directions,
along with compassion & kindness.
Somewhere is the nexus. I thought we both
stood in the same spot; now we are just owls
unsure of our relationship, forgetting everything
but the way sound travels in the dark night.

HUNGER & SNAKE

There are predators, of course—owls, hawks, raccoons—
so many things eat birds' eggs, hatchlings,
the unwary adults, but only the rat snake
constricts its way up even metal poles,
so people must install baffles or plastic nets
to confound them.

I saw a snake caught this way,
balled up in a net & thrashing.
It seeming to emerge
as if from a black cloud, body so black
against the black mesh,
but its mouth gaping white—

      a hole of sky opening in the middle
      of a bird swarm,
      the brilliant twilight
      radiating momentarily
      before their flying choked it closed.

WALKING PALMS UP IN THE DARK

Returning to the lake I'd thrown my wedding ring into,
someone whispered, *It's still there you know, undissolved.*

In the shrubs chipmunks scurried, & the man with the bottle
of Jim Beam sunned himself in the dirt path. He said he hears
voices in the winds, coming from all directions. I know this
because I hear them as well. His mouth was an O he raised
the bottle to; the bottle mouth was an O he poured himself into.

My hands were ears I used to locate myself through this dark.

JUNIPER

Once I heard a story of a woman
who carried snails under her breasts,
smuggling them to the Pure Land,
as if there were such a place,
as if any place were not. It was not the year
of the Great Flu—1918—an epidemic
my mother had been curious about
before she died, not quite a century late,
and just before the new epidemic,
her lungs also drowned.

I am drinking gin alone by a window
splashed with mud. Its transmuted berries
in my throat, belly, bloodstream,
spread like the strings of the super-cluster—
Laniakea, Hawaiian for "immense heaven."
Some galaxies, the scientists say, flow
toward the mystery "super attractor,"
while in another space, a juniper bush
is giving itself up to become a part of someone.

I have heard that snails heave their hushed bodies
up the Buddha, becoming a cap of protection,
for they know they can do so little alone.

I'm glad my mother is not alive
to hear a man insist on a wall around America.
One great war was ending when that flu ignited,
killing more then the war had. It was a year
of peace & death no one expected.
Another great war already fermenting.

Through the splattered window, I see
only the silhouettes of birds: blue jays,
swallows. That half the people want
a wall saddens me. Our immense heaven,

the scientists say, sidles up against another:
two minds or foreheads resting
touching, yet impenetrable, so much
bone & blood keeping us apart.

SATELLITES: PERMANENT ONLY IN MEMORY

While standing on my back porch leaning
into the night calling my dog home, a light

ball erupted over my head & streaked

a knife gash across the sky toward north.
I knew it couldn't be only a rock entering

our atmosphere, but something human-made—
both mighty & an achievement—breaking

apart when it lost its orbit. Someone said this

must be what happened to my husband—
that he'd come into my orbit once a long time

ago & lodged there, serenely circling as if
he were a natural body & the gravitational

pull a given, until something in his workings

clicked open or shut—can I say I actually recall
the day, how his eyelids closed & opened?

& what I saw was a shadow, a turning away—

     & so can you blame me if,
when this satellite descended above, my dog

not listening, again, instead wanting to smell

the leaves & soil damp from an earlier rain,
my instinct was to reach upwards
       with both hands
              as if to catch it?

THE WATER INSISTS ON TAKING EVERYTHING

        Each year
we pump sand from hundreds of yards beyond
the wrack to replenish our beaches.   Us
laying our bodies down each new season
as if this one might not end.   But the waves
        keep coming
& we still haven't figured out time.   This same
fly bit me dozens of times, each time me
        watching, letting
the slow pierce happen, the proboscis
        unfurl, hoping
to slap it dead before it could get away.   I lost
this game of concentration repeatedly.   Finally,
I stood, ready to plunge into the ocean, when my hands,
unbidden by my mind reacted to another sting.

The little black body against the borrowed sand.

I kicked it covered, unceremonial,
        but could have wept. Even now
        the water inside me wants to well,
        waves ready to break again on my shore.

CURVE OF FORGETTING

He said he should have just walked away
after sleeping with me that first time,
said, *Good luck,* & moved on. The anger
in his face, the way his eyes steeled.
He was recalling a moment he didn't act
over twenty years ago. I recall this while we're bombing
somewhere. A cruel man mad in power gassing people,
videos viral, children choking on their vomit.
We've known about this for years. The last
president having run on no troops, no military
intervention, the country exhausted, the next one
got to play hero, distract from his larger incompetence.
His ratings went up & up.   My husband texts
from his apartment, the one he's left us to live in.
Postponed walking away by a couple of decades,
& now it's worse. I can't tell whose fault
anything is anymore. Responsibility is easy
to assign when forgetting has thinned
the complexities, complicities. I don't know
if I love him or love the idea of love.
Does violence resolve violence? Whatever
I once knew, I seem to have forgotten.

DISSONANCE & STILL

Crows outside my window in the dancing trees
make me think of intergenerational trauma,
& in the distance a lone red-tailed hawk reminds
me of perspective though perspectivizing
may be just a way to not feel what I feel,
something the crows' caws & squawks
irritate me back to. All over the world
people are flocking—in protest or flight—
so much weather & greed. A terrifying gust,
& suddenly the crows are a-wing, all of them
instantly, like ink slashes across paper, this sky
studded, then they settle again. Those wings
withdrawn. Am I ashamed to be alone?
Embarrassed by our dissonance, I'm still
grateful for the crows' calls which insist
I not ignore what is happening. There is
still the sky & this paper we call living.

TRAFFIC & CONSTRUCTION

Rilke wrote *our heart*—almost, I could stop
there but I can never stop loving
you though I've tried. The thing that bothers me

is the strangeness of plural & singular
in the phrase *our heart is between hammers*
& wonder whether this is an error in translation

or Rilke's intention in German. Shouldn't it be
our hearts or *my heart?* I'm thinking
of our divorce, which happened

on a day I was lecturing in the very room we
held our wedding in. I'm embarrassed to say
I know something about suffering;

there is so much in the world I only know
of at a distance. Maybe this is the key
to *our heart.* Jack Gilbert wrote,

*We find out the heart only by dismantling what
the heart knows.* You swung a hammer
& took it all down. Not much has changed.

Yesterday after chips & guacamole with the kids,
you kissed me on the cheek, the kids cooing
that mom & dad are best friends now. My chest

a hollow where the hole was blown, hidden
by this civility. *We can break through marriage
into marriage,* Gilbert wrote. Someone drove

a truck through Times Square again that week.
It's old news now, & the day went on, tourists
watching to see how everyone behaved

after such a public violence. Traffic
& construction continuing, jack hammers
& blood, the city continuing to beat & beat.

EVERYONE IS WHAT

He tells me he is upset, sad, anxious. So
my anger slips sideways like shower steam.
When the bathroom door is opened, a cool
rush of sympathy clears the mirror. There I am!
Sympathy is safer than empathy sometimes.
Okay, I say to him, *breathe.* He has harmed me
terribly. No one would disagree if I turned away
from his suffering. He's so ashamed at what
he's done, but when I look in the mirror what
I see is everyone; I know what it is like
to walk inside a cloud of my own making.

MOLECULARITY

We're in trouble;
a hungry accident is about to happen,
            & what science there is might turn
            out to be what saves us from us;
            a hot bowl held in both hands
            the only way to mark time.

Conditionality is unconditional:
            brains plastic after all,
humans one example of plastic art,
            all tape & welding, sponge
                 & junk, glass & dried worms.
We sidle up to each other
            all bristle & solace—each the center of
                 our own art installation—our
            bones mellowing from red to yellow,
                & wanting to crack
                        each other open. Is this all?   Bones

                like planets,
                like the sea,

drawn by music & gravity,
            the hum of those cells being born
            or dying, brains seemingly set
            inside themselves, but really just waiting
            for some new event, catastrophe,
                a singularity weighty as a thick, fatty stew?

Babies have more red marrow   adults more yellow,
        though in instances of severe blood loss, yellow
        is elastic, reforming into red,
similar to scavengers cracking open carcasses,
        predators left behind, scooping marrow. Cheap
        protein, fulsome,
        but a way to go on.

IV
Marriage

(trajectories)

Last night, on the boardwalk in Asbury Park,
the couple went looking for their marriage
in the sea air. A young man suddenly came at them
from the side, screaming, *Your face makes me so angry,*
I want to smash it. He was glaring past them to someone
beyond as if they didn't exist, & their stride, the paced
one of a couple who've been together a long time,
carried them just beyond his trajectory, the balled bats
of his arms swooshing behind her back. She turned
on instinct, perhaps to intervene in the violence,
but her husband curled her into the space between
his body & hers, then twirled her back out ahead,
then forward, almost as if they'd been dancing.

(skin)

She was walking in the woods & saw them
coiled atop each other. On bottom, a large, thick milk snake
with bands of smoke & slate. On top—
thin, delicate, green, luminous—an emerald that darted away
as if caught doing something wrong.
She contemplated the remaining one a long while, on her haunches,
hands on knees, peering closely. Was it dead?
She thought to poke it & picked up a stick, but this seemed petty,
even selfish, & tossed the stick away.
The snake quivered, raising its head & tail. She wondered why
it had tolerated the other—had she been stealing
heat? But these were just snakes, & she knew they weren't lonely,
yet something like aloneness made her feel
profoundly present. Finally, she walked on, & it seemed she might
veer off the path, maybe even shed herself.

(intergenerational wounds)

A man is bending his wife; he is bending
her around something she has bent
herself around all her life. He learned
to do it well, but today, to his own surprise,
he admits to her he saw a good knife
the day before when they were at the flea market.
He says it is like one his uncle gave him as a boy,
& that, if she likes, he will get this knife—
one with a curved tip—& skin her
like she's never been skinned before.
Just keep bending me, she says.

(water)

His wedding ring slipped off one day in the rain.
He'd become as beautiful on the outside
as she always knew he was, so fit, skinny really—
running miles, rowing, eating better. He said
it was an accident, & kneel-walked along the road,
hands like baleen skimming the gutters. The storm
drains are labeled to deter people from dumping
oil & paint, for all water goes back to water.
There are whales who swim from one end
of the earth to the other yet never meet. For weeks,
he told her not to worry, he'd find what he'd lost.

(wood & dog)

It was getting close to chopping time,
but neither of them wanted to do it anymore,
him tired, her thinking it isn't her job,
both of them just wanting to get lost
in separate woods. Up the hill where the dog
likes to go, there's an abandoned wildcat bulldozer.
They have separate fantasies about starting
it up, what damage they might do—things
they are each ashamed of & can't imagine
sharing.   They've begun going up there
alone to pray, kneeling as before a god;
she wanting advice, him forgiveness,
but every time, a disappointment.

(after unseen damage from the flood)

The double trunked tree cracked, one side still reaching
to the sky, the other angled, all strangeness
& architectural drama, curving like an arm,
ending in a long green finger pointing toward the house
as if in accusation & some branches flicking the blades
below as if trying to pick up something dropped or lost.

(stew)

It takes about one rabbit per five people,
so you can imagine the number
of flayed bodies piled on the counter.
I was 26 & a bad cook, my mother's mother
having died before she taught her,
& these bodies looked real-bodied. I asked if he
could take them apart, but he said, if I was going to do it,
I should do it right. It was a rite of passage
making stew from scratch like that,
pots & pots of it. The house stunk.
You'd think I would have known better,
but that would require knowing oneself as a fool,
which no one ever seems able to do, a stew
that requires a long time, a good burn,
& a willingness to be chopped to pieces.

(roots)

When the tree with two trunks split that spring,
the roots giving way in the overburdened earth,
the upright one looked younger, more vulnerable,
& they waited to see if the other half would die.
He cut the dead branches; she packed new soil
in a mound between the trunks planting
perennials—cone flower, bee balm, verbena—
to protect them & forestall more erosion.
They watered & watered & stood blinking
on the street, sweaty & blinded & wondering.

(the re-articulation)

In her travels, she came to a bridge
made entirely of bones, each carved with a small number
offering the promise of sequence.
An old need for orderliness asserted itself.
First, she took the non-weight bearing bones,
laying them in small piles along the shore.
This went well until she started to take apart the span,
& things fell apart. She'd only wanted to find out
what mystery creature it had once been.
Still, she persevered, considering what she'd need
to do this right, making a list: no children to distract her,
or a husband, no job even, certainly not a career.
She could not go back on the path she'd come,
knowing as she did what & who was behind her,
& couldn't go forward because she'd dismantled
the bridge. Instead, looking across the river
hands on her hips, she said, *I'll just stay right where I am.*

(woman with two hearts)

One of her two hearts is dying,
the other thriving. She doesn't have a clock
for any of this. Somewhere a crevasse
opens wide near a glacier; a breach
lets contained water out. Once a man
knew about a wilderness he wanted
to explore. He told her winter involves
a little dying, a little staying alive.
He was leaving, he said.
She would have ripped one heart out
to have kept him from going. She would
have ripped out the other to have gone along.

(how to hold a heart)

As if lifting cupped hands to drink,
or roasted duck, an owl's feathers, beak
to cheek. Not like an apple or a baseball.
A lost thing in mud found. A blessing
in the surf you cast yourself into; a dying
face that still has bones. The way you try
to recall details of a dream, not grasping.
A wafting on the air leading you somewhere
you didn't know you needed to go. Memory
in flesh. Not with your hands at all; with
your own muscle, everything you own.

(more than mercy)

Scientists ask whether light chooses
between being a wave or a particle. Sometimes
we choose for it, they say, assigning
it one or the other, making reality dense
with perception, which is only temporary.
When particles meet, they are forever connected;
even separated, they affect each other no matter
how far apart they become. In one story, there
is poison in a wound; in another, we are just
asking to see under the surfaces of this world.

(what they try in spring)

They were hoping to stay married, & she'd said,
We love our lost, a strange Spoonerism, but also true.
He laughed with rue, said, *So much seems lost: art, planes, people.*
They lay in the grass, feet touching at the toes, pleased
to watch the kids shoot each other with pistols, throw
fistfuls of water into the air. They might have wanted
to hold each other, but for the thousand blades between.

(being in becoming)

> *I knew you would be lovely, a lane of flowering trees in a man's form.*
> Alicia Ostriker

Everything falls away & the animal becomes
the anti-animal, the spirit dissipates. Easy to feel
lost & alone. Necessary. No one completes
the other for long. Half man, half woman,
shadows seen best when the sun is at zenith,
& then one of them must go into the water
for the other & then the other must claw out
of the quicksand & burn for them both.
On any journey there is exhaustion, & you
might run out of food & have to ride hungry,
the famine of the body having to be born
because you have eaten everything there is.

(motel)

Inland, just west of Atlantic City,
old motels stand hunched as if ashamed,
the people inside propping them up.
No one told me about the architecture
of sorrow, how expensive it is to build,
how long it takes to tear down.
East as far as you can go here in New Jersey
is the ocean in which swimming
& drowning sometimes look the same.

V
Fallen Kingdoms

A Guide to Wild Flowers

Early in the marriage, he gave me an old book,
    saturated colors of the plates
    as thinned as the marriage
later became.   The names of flowers so romantic—
Bee Balm, Mad Dog Scullcap, Monkey-Flower—
& some are poisonous—
              Sweet Pea, Buttercup, even Daffodil,
                  which, if enough ingested, can kill you.
There are also plants that can cure sick landscapes
& factory grounds, absorbing arsenic & mercury.
I wonder what happens to the laden roots; is toxicity

merely transferred from one place to another?

The inscription reads,
    To what we will grow together, Love Always.

But so much grows wild & after twenty years—
roots knotted, soil eroded—we still reach
    but know neither of us is the sun.

The potted Calla lily kills hundreds of cats a year,
yet its rhizomes can be crushed into a caustic flour
for a passable bread. If this seems strange, even dangerous,
perhaps we have to feed each other whatever we have
        when we have nothing else left to give?

THE LOGIC OF YOU

When you wrote of torture, the ineffectual
& desperate grandfathers of history, lost
fathers drowned in their own torments, feminism
& the eco-poetics of Lopez, et al., I never looked
at the loose threads of your wrists,
what was about to become undone, the inadequacy
of love's logic.   I wonder if love
resides in some fascia between entities, this universe
held together by the unknowable. Someone told me
my worst fault was desire
to have
answers. Isn't that what logic attempts
to provide? Or at least a template for testing truth?
             In truth I only know I loved
                       you.   But something
happened to me. To us. Until something
else happened to you, & the logic of you
changed like a blown circuit.

They say trauma is held in the body's fascia
making it inflexible, even brittle,   &
maybe like the big guts of some older men,
shredded inside, hernias in the abdomen
letting all the innards push out. Some call it
beer belly. I always think they look pregnant
with something they don't know
how to give birth to.

KINGDOM OF CLASS

All I wanted was love, really, & thought that was
what everyone wanted; what a fool I was for love.
But really, that became security, & that attack,
that day I saw those towers—
we all saw them—go down in a white flurry
of hurricane dust in the city the world loves, neighborhoods
plumed in billows, we just watched & then brought home
our own dead. Next the neighbors all lost
their jobs, & we started taking all those pay cuts
& hoped our AC made it another season
& the roof another year.   Love
is a kind of capital, as is eros, & some days I still believe
you can have your eros & eat it, too, but that Jersey rock star
opened the soup kitchen in town, & a friend said,
Why don't we try it, you know, just because.
She's out of work & her spouse hasn't had a new account
in months, & I think her family might need that meal.

Sometimes, I just want to touch people, so I steal
caresses—an arm, a sleeve. I touch my screens, people
all over the world a text away keeping me from filling my pockets
with old hard drives & walking into the ocean.

When did we forget what we all wanted
& settle for what we got? I'm trying not to go to sleep again.
Instead, I'll try to stay awake in the tomorrow
of the future where we all hope our children
will have it easier & better, richer & more wonderful
than we've had, better than anyone else ever had,
as if it is possible to protect anyone from anything at all.

THE WILL

The nurse tells me his wife is one, as well,
& at home, they argue over who should serve
the other; they are both tired of caring for bodies
not their own. My heart got close to breaking
a second time, its clock gone wonky,
someone inside knocking against
the bone cage demanding release.

It's late, close to his shift's end;
one more blood draw, he's out of here.
A baby is squalling. Every whisper in the hall
has some version of *sorry* in it.
       My husband is leaving me,
        says his heart is a twisted tuba.
I've been asking him to stay. Now, I tell him to go, but it is simply
home to the kids. Without them, the fascia holding the organs
of us together will unbuckle & fall away.

In the pall of artificial light, assaulted subtly by the TV,
I grip the rail of this bed as if it is a boat upon which my body
has been set fire. Will anyone believe me if I say there is joy
in burning to a cinder, that what incinerates isn't me at all,
but what I am in service to? What a pretty word, *serve,*
better than *sorry,* & one way to tame
the wild animal clambering
for its own sake: feeding it
what it wants by feeding it
to others.

MUSIC IN THE KINGDOM OF THE HEART

In the echocardiogram, the muscle looks
like a human drumming, though the technician
holding the transducer to my chest, merely chuckles
when I tell her this. Maybe after seeing a thousand
of these muscles close up, she is inured to their natures,
her job being to look for what is flawed or broken.

When I think of a pump & valves, it sounds
like an engine, but the whirl in me is more
than machine: the sonic arms of valves thrust open
& bang closed with a kind of music, as if life
depended on rhythm. Which of course it does.

I used to be a drummer, but was no good. Still,
I tell the technician the old drumming joke:
There are three kinds of drummers, I say,
those who can count & those who can't.

Sometimes I experienced the "drummer's high,"
which neuroscientists explain as the measurable
unity between brains in the act of collaboration.
& sometimes even a weary somatic metaphor
makes a person's feeling clear: my heart is broken.
Maybe the issue is that even in married life,
I thought one plus one equaled one.

Soon, they will cut a small hole in my thigh,
snake a camera into my femoral artery up my torso
in order to see the drummer under my left breast
who thrums so wildly, & look for evidence
of what went wrong, which they will not find.

Hold still, the tech says & moves the wand
around, *We're almost through*, echoing
what he'd said: *We're through*.

Bonne Chute (good falling)

Fall has always seemed like a beginning to me—
of school, holidays, structure after the looseness
& wonder of summer—& this fall, a year after
he said he would move out, & then did, telling me
we will divorce whether I agreed or not, I am thinking
how we used to thrill at an early snow scatter,
always saying, *Bon Hiver*, French for *Good Winter*,
to each other, late in fall after the saw-buzzing
of cicadas & the shuttering of dried leaves into bag
after bag was through. Once he told me:
   Winter is a little dying,
   a little holding on until spring.

Now I wonder if surviving is sufficient, if, instead
of dying, living is really about letting go, a little falling
over & over into whatever comes next.

HEAT

Rovelli writes the difference
between the past & the future exists

only when there is heat. I like to watch
your body in the present. It makes me

know something about being here
inside this one, bowl of hips both

full & empty, a heat making tomorrow
possible for me, though watching you

& the dip of arm as bow against the violin
of the other appendage—also arm—there

is no sound but the heat slipping down
the body through breath.   Is sound

a kind of heat? Sympathetic vibration
across energy that, when dense, is matter?

What is the matter, I want to ask? Do I
want to ask? As it's apparent in your body,

at least in this moment, which isn't the past
or future. Do you want to burn? I once did,

wanted to & also did, burning my way out
of memories into a future I didn't know

was possible but longed for. Is longing a kind
of heat? Rovelli writes that *in every case*

in which heat exchange does not occur...we see
the future behave exactly like the past.

When I push my hands against you, I'll offer
what can burn. When I step back, will you ignite

me, please? I want to know what next is
possible, what is possibly next; I imagine

hearing some bell in an incendiary future
we can only seem to sound our way toward.

ALMOST NOTHING SOMETHING
[stars / plates / cells]

An earthquake two states over,
         & here
nothing,   my heart
steadier & louder
then it's been in a while.   Desire
in the interstices almost worn away,
so everything grates, tectonic.
Two people cried in front
of me today, one in shame,
one in gratitude: one apologized
for being human—what a feat—
& I'd simply absorbed the shocks
of them, moistened myself
by their brave vulnerabilities,
for a moment,   the plates
shifting against each other
with a little less pain.   Someone
posted on Twitter their cat
leaped; another their house
swayed.   Nothing is provable.
I think for a moment, when I go
home, I'll wrap my arms across
my chest bones,   try to feel
my own invisible muscle
& think about forgiveness,
but that's not what's happening.

I find myself thinking instead
of the word *tectonic* which in geology
refers to the energy, processes, structures
that make the earth the earth—then, now, someday—
the plates sliding over its crust,
how mountains
grow, erode, how living beings become fossils
becoming fuel for other living beings,
an ethical question leading me to *architectonics,*
& those who mine
structures of thought—Aristotle, Kant, Foucault—

which will lead me to think
about why it's easier to think
than feel sometimes, & I'll wonder
about that person's sensitive cat,
or the person sensing the sheer in the bones
of their house, & whether those who study
cytoarchitectonics—slicing & staining
slivers of brains to learn
how neurons create constellations, stars, & universes
inside
the plates of our skulls—ever find themselves weeping

as I am at the counter as I peel this hard boiled egg,
its shell not slipping off elegantly, but in bitter
unreleasing bits I must dig at
with the nail
of my smallest finger.   One crier—
have you ever heard that phrase: *I had a crier today?*—
was apologizing; the other
was begging
for something that wouldn't relieve the real stresses

rippling through the firmament of her life.
All I could do was lean forward
in my chair, meet her
gaze & witness
the light years' echo of explosions
still percussing in her life & the ones manifesting
right then, just then—shall I recount them?—
alcoholic stepfather, evictions, lost job, depressed mother;
Old stories always a new shock. Could I tell her
there is a universe inside her, stars?   I could.   I did.

But I'm tired & suspicious of poetry—Gilbert, Levine, Dunn—
& Glück's *Faithful & Virtuous Night* reeks
like some tar pit I might fall into, sucked down
where my bones might fossilize, the only real residue
back there in the gaze between me & *a crier,*
something like nothing, but *surely something*
passing
in the seemingly empty space
between the plates
of us.

Acknowledgments

The Aurorean "Dissonance & Still"

Blackbird "Icarus in the House of Spirits," & "The Troubles of Men: Holometaboly"

The Brooklyn Review "Women & Other Hostages"

Cimarron Review "Marriage (Being in Becoming)"

Deluge "Marriage (stew)," "Marriage (the re-articulation)," "Marriage (woman with two hearts)," & "Marriage (how to hold a heart)"

Diode "Marriage (trajectories)" & "The Public Pool"

Fjords Review "Marriage (skin)"

Folio: A Literary Journal at American University "You Have to Become Stone"

Gamut "The Will"

Green Mountains Review "Emoticonsficated"

Guernica "Molecularity"

The Kenyon Review Blog "Bonne Chute (good falling)"

The Literary Review "Women & the Syntactical World"

Massachusetts Review "Music in the Kingdom of the Heart"

Mortar Magazine "Satellite: Permanent Only In Memory" & "The Owls of Mercy & Grace"

North American Poetry Review "Kingdom of Class"

Pank Magazine "Some Linguists See Syntax as a Branch of Biology" & "Women & the Natural World"

Pebble Lake Review "Sweet Sick"

Philadelphia Review of Books "Credit Rating"

Plume "Hunger & Snake"

Poets & Artists: The Male Muse Issue "What Comes Out of the Sky at a Horizontal Trajectory", "Marriage (Water)", "The Places We Have All Been"

Posit: A Journal of Literature & Art "Marriage (motel)" "Marriage (intergenerational wounds)" "Marriage (wood & dog)" & "Marriage (roots)"

Prairie Schooner "The water insists on taking everything"

RipRap Literary Journal "Until You Know It"

Solstice "Traffic & Construction" & "Everyone is What"

South Florida Poetry Journal "Medusa as a Parable of Faith & Resilience"

Spoon River "Biology Lesson: An Appropriation of the Lover"

SWWIM "Heat"

Tab: the journal of poetry and poetics "Marriage (more than mercy)

Tinderbox Journal "Walking Palms Up in the Dark" & "Juniper"

Whimperbang "Women & Other Female Identifications" & "Heat & Shame"

Women's Review of Books "Beneficial Insects"

Yes Poetry Magazine "Curve of Forgetting"

Gratitudes:

There are so many. Certainly, thank you to the editors at the journals & magazines who published poems from this collection before it cohered into a collection. This book began not long after my mother died & shortly after my husband left me when I had a heart attack. I didn't think I was going to be writing a book, & earlier versions had to be thrown away. One of Robert Frost's dictums is that we need to write from grief, not grievance. Both are real & important, yet neither are simple to write about; the former can be sentimental, the latter didactic, and one's own culpability is perhaps hardest to stand.

Hence, the many gratitudes are because even though I did continue to write through breakage, I could not have re-cohered, let alone survived, without the people I'm going to list. There will be people I miss, & I anticipate that with regret, so I preface this by saying it's rarely the people who hurt us who can heal us, but I also don't know that we can heal alone; perhaps we need community, need friends, need to witness for each other, need to allow others to help us when we break. In the main, it was the women who came forward in my life, the deepening of older relationships, the generosity of colleagues, as well as sisters in writing, the new friendships that miraculously emerged that have been the line I held to as I was dragged from the rubble of my life—mother's death; husband's desertion; children's launches—back to the light. As well, there were other people & communities that became caissons in the construction of my new life.

The gift in grief, a phrase taken from the title of a book one of the women listed below once gave me, is not singular. There are many, not least of which is the possibility of embodying ourselves more fully in interaction with others: if we can avoid calcifying into fear and unprocessed pain, we can become more open to joy; if we can understand the failings and frailties of others, as well as ourselves, we can become kinder, more compassionate. In vulnerability, we deepen our capacity for wisdom. Accountability & rectification co-exist but are only part of the coordinates of restitution that may fall to our own reanimation after loss. If we let down the false armor of our defendedness, we may be less arrogant, more genuine, and maybe more open to what could not be imagined as possible.

As I turn 60, I know this decade to have been the most painful in my life, & the questions it generated about mercy and forgiveness are still unanswered—but it has been amazing, as well, & to the many, many writers, artists, musicians, colleagues, students, neighbors, & friends that have been willing to talk about your own griefs, betrayals, & losses, your bewilderment & discoveries, the shames, guilts, & redemptions, the one-foot-in-front-of-the-others in this great going on, even during your own brutal dark nights, sharing the notes of your songs, laughter, weeping with my own, I thank you. I couldn't have done it—whatever *that* is—without the light each of you is in the world.

To Stephen Dunn (for years & years of love & good talk) who weighed in on some of these poems, especially the marriage cycle.

To Mihaela Moscaliuc and Michael Waters, special thanks for the good poetry fellowship, the music, the Asbury Park beach sunset talks.

To Tony Hoagland (you are missed) for his comments on some of these poems, the many talks about poetry, and for introducing me to the GMNF community.

To brothers in different realms in my life: BJ Ward, Jeff Ford, Kurt Scheffler, Alex Idavoy, & especially Brandon Gramer. Interventions. Fierce jokes. No bullshit. Speaking from truth.

To Keith H. & Tom D., laughter during tears, all around. *"Oh, l'amour, l'amour, how it can let you down. Hmm. How it can pick you up again."* From *The Women*

To Ray G., Andrew P., George M., way-finders, music-makers, light-bringers.

To Tony P., onstage, backstage, or down front: *"For what it's worth, I never stole from anybody who would go hungry."* From *To Catch a Thief*

To Project Write Now (Jennifer, Greg, Allison, Lisa, Gay, & Ray), thank you for the work you do & for letting me be part of the team for a while.

To Terry Donahue, Tara Tomaino, Luke Johnson, & Kate De Lancelotti, writers, wave-makers, word-wrights.

To my Sierra Nevada University MFA family: director, Brian Turner, & all the fellow faculty & fantastic writers, especially gal-pals June Sylvester Saraceno, Gayle Brandeis, Rebecca Makkai, Gailmarie Pahmeier, Patricia Smith, plus Benjamin Busch and Lee Herrick: conversations with each of you—about our work as well as this work of living—has sustained me, & some of these poems were written or revised on the shores of Lake Tahoe during residencies.

To the Great Mother New Father Conference folk: well, many of these poems were written on the shores of your lake, as well, literally & metaphorically, & you know what it means when ten thousand crows land on your roof. There are too many of you to name. What did T. say? There's a Rumi outbreak in the wild woods of Maine? May I get lost with you in those woods for a long time, & I'll always hold a tiny piece of the "beauty is begun" that you all spin with your voices, art, poetry, music, & good will: drums in the night calling, calling.

To Eileen. Beth. Carolina. Mary. Sue. Meg. Colleen. Donna. Dara. Janice. Girlfriends. Each of you, the most ethical women I know, and Oh, what you know about Hostages to Fortune, yet you bring bright lights into the woods we all walk through. Our talks, your creative manifestations, the little survivings, & the willingness to share the hows of that...

To Chelsea. Following your gifts through your own grief; thank you for your survivorship, intelligence, vision.

To Leslie. Woman! Beneath the bright eye of the moon, we walked out of the dark into the mornings of lives we are re-making.

To Renee Ashley, with an eye like an arrow, heart like a rubber duck on the ocean, & a laugh that goes with both. I wish you wombats.

To Karen, who makes grace look easy & without whom this drumming heart couldn't have kept beating again after it crashed, you unweave and tease out the woof and warp of a thing & do so with a gentleness that is unparalleled, but I know is hard won.

To Kathy Graber, faithful sister in the word & the world as we held each other's hands through some dark woods & talked each other across some ledges, just saying...

To my still-here kinfolk: Dad & step-mom, Bill & Sue, step dad, Russell (& Ray & his whole crew of good humans), siblings Steven, Shimmee (& Wes), Zach, Melissa (& Charlie), & Russell (& Theresa), Aunts Adele & Judy, Uncle Marty & cousins Kim (& Kevin), Diane, Mark, Eric (& their various kids & Arizona crew) & other cousins, Nan, Kate, Stephanie, Geneva, Vanessa, Patty, Margo, Ciara, & Nelson, and Gerard (& the whole Florida crew). And to my no longer-here folk, I won't name you today, but you're not forgotten.

To my kids, my exes: each of you is on your own journey, & the ways we have loved & hurt each other speak to the complexities of family & how love really is never enough. Or maybe just not the whole story. If I've failed you—& I know I have—know I wish I could have done better by each of you—loved you longer or harder, given what you needed or wanted—& my poems are a record, if nothing else, of the striving to understand you, us, this work of endless becoming, & the salvaging of what I could from the various wrecks; we are all hostages in some way.

To Diane Goettel, editor & publisher of Black Lawrence Press (& the wonderful team she has assembled over the years, especially Kit Frick, Yvonne Garrett, and the rockstar, Angela Leroux-Lindsey, & others behind the scenes I know less well but who keep up the work of a press), you have supported my work—even sometimes saying no to a manuscript that wasn't right or ready—thank you for all you do for writers and the effort to curate & make sense of our world.

Finally, to EVT, who came in on the tail end of this project (& has sparked much work toward the next) & with whom I landed in lock down, so much music in the interstices between we, so much wind & water yet to navigate. My mom used to say that grace is seeing in someone's face the child they once were. Here's to doing that for each other.

This book is dedicated to Emory Yun-hsi Broek

Photo: Emory Brock

Laura McCullough's newest book of poems is *Women & Other Hostages* (Black Lawrence Press, 2021). Her previous books from Black Lawrence Press are *Jersey Mercy*, *Rigger Death & Hoist Another*, and *Speech Acts*. Her other books include *The Wild Night Dress*, selected by Billy Collins for the Miller Williams Poetry Series (University of Arkansas Press, 2017), *Panic* (winner of the Kinereth Kensler Award, Alice James Books, 2009), and *What Men Want* (XOXOX Press). She is the editor of two anthologies, *A Sense of Regard: Essays on Poetry and Race* (University of Georgia Press) and *The Room and the World: Essays on Stephen Dunn* (Syracuse University Press). Her work has appeared in *Best American Poetry*, *Georgia Review*, *American Poetry Review*, *The Writer's Chronicle*, *Guernica*, *The Southern Review*, *Gulf Coast*, *Pank*, *Hotel America*, *Prairie Schooner*, and many other journals and magazines. She has had scholarships or fellowships to the Bread Loaf Writers Conference, the Nebraska Summer Writers Conference, Sewanee Writers Conference, the Vermont Studio Center, the Virginia Center for the Arts, and has been a Dodge Poetry Festival poet, a Florida Writers Circuit poet, and a Decatur Book Festival poet. She has had three NJ State Arts Council Fellowships, two in poetry and one in prose. She received her MFA from Goddard College and teaches full time at Brookdale Community College in NJ where she founded the Creative Writing Program and is on the faculty of the Sierra Nevada low-res MFA and has taught for Ramapo College and Stockton University. Visit her at www.lauramccullough.org